CHINA
A NEW REVOLUTION?

JOHN BRADLEY

A WATTS/GLOUCESTER BOOK

Contents

▷ In 1949 the communists came to power in China. To remember all those who died fighting to achieve this victory the communists have built monuments throughout China.

The People's Republic of China has just celebrated 40 years of existence. The occasion was completely overshadowed by events in Tiananmen Square, Beijing, when at least 1,000 civilians were massacred by troops in June 1989. China has always been a puzzle to the outside world. From very early on, it was inaccessible because of vast deserts to the north, the highest plateau in the world to the southwest and seas to the south and east. For centuries it was technologically advanced: in the 1st century paper was invented; and in the 8th century printing and gunpowder were invented. But by the 18th century China had fallen behind some European countries.

China is the world's third largest country after Canada and the Soviet Union. It covers an area of nearly 9,560,900 sq km and is divided into 22 provinces, five self-governing regions and three municipalities which are ruled directly by central government. Nearly three-fifths of its land is mountain, desert and water. The North China Plain is an important wheat-producing area. Central and southern China are both very fertile regions and produce much of the country's wheat, millet, cotton, rice and tea. China has many natural resources including reserves of iron, coal, oil and natural gas. It produces tungsten, antimony, nickel, copper, lead and zinc. China has chemical, textile, metal and engineering industries.

China is the world's most populous country. It has over 1,045 million inhabitants. Although China has the world's second largest city, Shanghai, with 12 million people, 63 per cent of its people live in the countryside. Its population had grown so much from 1949-79, that it has strict birth control laws. Since 1980 the government has encouraged Chinese couples to have only one child.

Over 93 per cent of the people of China belong to the Han nationality. The remaining seven per cent belong to 55 different ethnic groups. These include Mongolians, Manchus, Tibetans, Uighurs and the Miaos. They have their own languages, traditions and religions.

Since 1949 China has had a communist system of government. This means the leading members of the Communist Party run the country. More than 48 million people are members – only four per cent of the population. They are a privileged group. The leading members of the party have for some time been an elderly group of men. They take their decisions in great secrecy. The Communist Party is riddled with corruption but is very powerful because the army supports it.

The communist victory

China has seen upheavals and transformations as the ancient civilisation has come into contact with the modern Western world. After a civil war the communists emerged victorious.

△ The Great Wall of China is almost 2,000 years old and it runs for thousands of kilometres through extremely rugged country. It was a real feat of engineering and a perfect example of how advanced the Chinese were at the time.

The present Chinese civilisation can be traced back to 5,000 years BC. It has survived and developed, however haltingly, to the present day. Thus the Chinese script of modern printed books and newspapers goes back nearly 4,000 years.

Up to 1911, the fall of the Qing dynasty, no Chinese was considered educated if he or she did not steep his or her mind in the philosophy of Kong Zi (known as Confucius). Kong Zi lived from 551 to 479 BC. His ideas were very conservative in that he taught that everyone had his or her place in the world and should respect the people above. Kong Zi thought rulers should be virtuous and benevolent or they would lose their power.

One surprising aspect of the present communist system is that it is roughly equivalent to the system installed by the first Emperor Qin Shihuang in 221 BC. He unified China with his army and forced people to move from one area to another. He divided the empire into 36 provinces ruled by civil and military governors and special superintendents; he also standardised written characters as well as laws, weights and measures. He ordered the building of a road system.

A self-sufficient empire

To protect themselves from foreign invaders the Chinese built the Great Wall. The Chinese Empire was very self-sufficient and the Great Wall did not prevent contact with the outside world. There were two established trade routes and the empire came under foreign rule several times. By the 8th century foreign religions, such as Islam, Buddhism and Nestorian Christianity, had been introduced. All these influences were absorbed.

At the time of the Roman Empire the Han dynasty already ruled some 60 million people. Apart from periods of anarchy or conquest, the Chinese people engaged in farming and were ruled by an emperor.

This huge empire did not go through the industrial revolution which transformed Europe in the 18th and 19th centuries. Once China had been technologically in advance of the rest of the world but she became backward. Thus by the 19th century parts of the weakened empire were occupied by European countries anxious for trade and other business opportunities.

The end of imperial China

The foreigners were very keen to trade in silk, tea and porcelain. They saw that there was a ruling, wealthy elite which could be seen as equivalent to the European ruling elite. However there was a marked difference between the ruling elite and the peasants. There was mass poverty in the countryside. Rebellions and a corrupt government combined with foreign intervention finally brought down the imperial system in 1911.

The problems facing China were immense. The country had to be defended as foreign countries, such as Russia to the north, were keen to annex territory. Another problem was how to overcome natural disasters and make sure there was enough grain to feed the people.

By the 1920s the nationalist and communist movements began to compete for power and influence in China. Both movements were influenced by ideas from France, Germany and the United States but gradually turned to the Soviet Union, which had had a communist revolution in 1917. Both the nationalists and the communists favoured socialist ideas but they disagreed on how quickly China could be transformed. The communists favoured a radical break with the past – a new beginning, while the nationalists wanted to improve the traditional way of life gradually – slow modernisation.

▽ A drawing showing the two great Chinese philosophers, Kong Zi and Lao Zi. Kong Zi's teachings have had a profound influence on Chinese thinking.

Sun Yatsen
In 1912 the small, but influential, nationalist movement came to power and a republic was proclaimed. Though the republic lasted until 1949 it was not united and had innumerable problems. Dr Sun Yatsen, the leader of the revolutionary alliance *Tongmenghui*, became the provisional president of the republic in 1912 and he publicly announced his way of solving China's problems. He would introduce moderate nationalism, and have a democratic system of government in which the people would have some say by electing the government. The main aim of the government would be the end of mass poverty.

However, within a year Sun Yatsen abdicated in favour of General Yuan Shikai, who had the support of the imperialists, who wanted to restore the empire. Shortly afterwards Yuan declared himself emperor. In 1916 Yuan died and local warlords (rich military leaders) seized power in many regions.

The warlords prevented urgent agricultural reforms, indeed any reforms, being carried out by Dr Sun's party, the *Guomindang*. By Sun's death in 1925 none of his magnificent programme of 1912 had been achieved.

△ Dr Sun Yatsen believed that nationalism should go with democracy and socialism. He wanted China to have a system of government, where the people could elect their own leaders.

The *Guomindang*
Sun's successor as leader of the *Guomindang* was General Chiang Kaishek, who was much more interested in power than in Dr Sun's principles. He had spent four months in the Soviet Union and did not like what he saw there. He was a military leader and in 1926 he led his troops on the "Northern Expedition" against the warlords. Within two years he had either defeated them or convinced them to join the *Guomindang*.

By 1928 Chiang was proclaimed the president of the Chinese Republic, even though he only controlled part of it. He set up his government in Nanjing. Backed by an army and supported by bankers and businessmen, he was a military dictator but he faced opposition from the communists. In the ensuing civil war and communist uprisings, the Chinese peasants' living conditions became even worse.

The conditions of the emerging working class – workers living in the cities – were no better. There was widespread use of children in businesses, wages were miserably low and working conditions unsafe and unbearable. It appeared that only the communists cared about the misery of the Chinese masses.

△ Chiang Kaishek was Sun Yatsen's chief of staff. He was a soldier who hated the communists and wanted to destroy them. He set up his own nationalist government but this proved to be corrupt.

△ Chinese communist strikers lead a demonstration in Shanghai in 1926. During the 1920s the communists quickly gained supporters.

The Chinese Communist Party

The Chinese Communist Party (CCP) was founded in 1921 by Chinese thinkers and intellectuals, such as professors Li Dazhao and Chen Duxiu. Mao Zedong was also a founding member. In 1927 General Chiang decided to attack several CCP strongholds. He used his troops to massacre thousands of communist members, particularly in Guangzhou and Shanghai. The communist leaders had decided that they would be more likely to succeed if they based their revolution on the peasants rather than city workers. The signal went out for a peasant uprising called "Autumn Harvest", in Mao's native province, Hunan. It was cruelly suppressed by Chiang's troops.

In the early and mid-1930s Chiang led five campaigns against the communist peasant Red Army. But the communists always escaped and in 1935 established themselves, after the famous "Long March", in Yanan in Shaanxi province. By then Mao was their new leader.

MONGOLIA
MANCHURIA
CHINA
KOREA
Beijing
Yanan
Shanghai
Changsha
HUNAN
Guangzhou
INDOCHINA

Japanese control from 1932
Principal communist bases
Japanese occupied area 1937-45
The Long March

◁ The Long March covered a distance of 10,000 km. Mao took his men through rough terrain to avoid the nationalists.

△ A Chinese nationalist poster produced in 1938 to encourage resistance to the Japanese. Chiang had to make peace with Mao after the Japanese invasion.

The Japanese invasions

Taking advantage of the continual civil war in China the Japanese Kwantung army seized Manchuria (Liaoning, Jilin and Heilongjiang provinces) in 1931. In 1933 they invaded southern China. Chiang considered the communists a worse threat to China than the Japanese. Many Chinese leaders felt that the communists and the nationalists should form a popular front to defeat the Japanese. General Chiang was reluctant to do this but in 1937 he was kidnapped by his officers and forced to sign an agreement with the communists. Most Chinese people wanted the Japanese out of their country and turned to Mao and his army.

The Japanese defeated both forces in the field and soon occupied the more prosperous eastern provinces. However, in 1941 Japan declared war on the Western Allies – the United States and Great Britain. During the Second World War, the British and later the Americans supplied General Chiang with war materials because China had joined the Allies. Mao's Red Army continued the fight against the Japanese. By this time Mao had fully developed his ideas on building a communist revolution. He had set up bases in remote parts of the country and was busy convincing peasants that the communists would help them. The communists also became expert in guerrilla warfare – from remote bases they would harass the nationalists.

▽ Mao in Yanan after the Long March. In this remote part of China Mao rebuilt the Communist Party.

After the Second World War

During the war there was a sort of truce between the nationalists and the communists. After the war ended in 1945, the Americans were anxious that the communists would not gain control of the country and put pressure on Chiang to form a coalition government. Chiang had some four million armed men with tanks, artillery and 1,000 aircraft, and an American promise of some $6,000 million worth of aid. He decided to fight the communists.

However, Mao's armies had also benefitted from the end of war. They were based in the north in Yanan, Shandong and Manchuria and seized arms, mostly light ones, abandoned by the retreating Japanese armies. Since neither side trusted the other, it was no surprise that both sides decided to fight it out. In 1946 civil war began again, when Chiang launched his troops in a three-pronged attack against the communist controlled provinces. With American help, Chiang airlifted some of his forces into the important cities and railway junctions of the north. Mao's troops avoided pitched battles and were able to counter Chiang's offensives. The communists simply cut off Chiang's troops in the north so they ran out of supplies and arms. By 1947 General Lin Biao organised the Red Army into the People's Liberation Army (PLA), but he only had about a third of the number of *Guomindang* forces.

△ Lin Biao organised the People's Liberation Army. In the communist government he became Minister of Defence.

▽ US Marines on a victory parade in Tianjin, October 1945. The United States sent Chiang equipment and supplies during the Second World War.

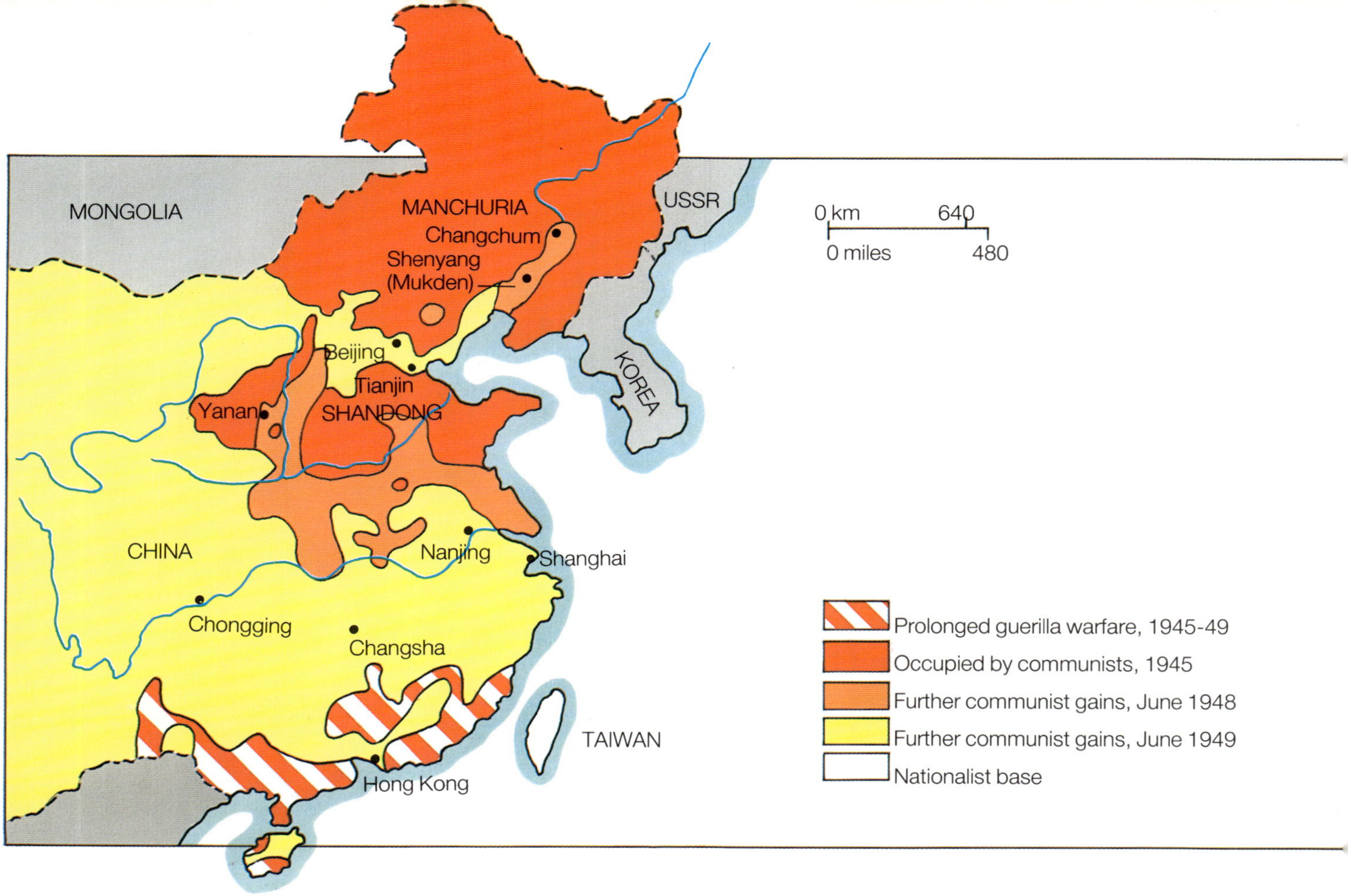

MONGOLIA
MANCHURIA
USSR
Changchum
Shenyang (Mukden)
KOREA
Beijing
Tianjin
Yanan
SHANDONG
CHINA
Nanjing
Shanghai
Chongqing
Changsha
TAIWAN
Hong Kong

0 km 640
0 miles 480

Prolonged guerilla warfare, 1945-49
Occupied by communists, 1945
Further communist gains, June 1948
Further communist gains, June 1949
Nationalist base

Nationalist problems

However, Chiang's immense army was most reluctant to fight the communists. During the offensive in Yanan some 20 soldiers deserted every day. The nationalist officers had to terrorise their troops to keep them in the fight. As soon as the officers absented themselves, the men deserted. Sometimes they also mutinied and killed their officers.

Chiang's nationalists had also succeeded in alienating the Chinese people. The nationalists were known to be very corrupt. General Chiang was a weak leader. He continually dismissed ministers and generals, but this did not make any difference. The massive input of American money somehow disappeared into the pockets of corrupt nationalist officials. This led to rising prices and inflation.

By contrast Mao's forces were well-disciplined, united and loyal. They made a point of distributing the money and food they conquered as soon as they took a territory from the nationalists. They encouraged the peasants to seize land and the communist troops practised selective killings, mainly of unpopular landowners and factory owners. In 1948 Mao staged uprisings all over China. General Lin led his armies on offensives and the *Guomindang* forces did not stop retreating. One by one the demoralised nationalist garrisons surrendered as they ran out of supplies.

◁ As soon as the Second World War was over, the civil war between the communists and the nationalists started up again. From bases in the north of China, the communists gradually extended their control of the country. Although the nationalists held the important centres of population in 1946, by 1948 they were imprisoned in the cities. The communists controlled the countryside and lines of communications. The communists then systematically took the cities and defeated the nationalists.

Victory

On 2 November 1948 Mukden (present-day Shenyang), an important railway crossing, was under Mao's control and Chiang had lost some 500,000 men. The communists reconquered the important Shandong province and in the battle of Huai-hai, Chiang lost another half a million men and much prestige.

This left northern China open to the PLA and Beijing fell to the communists in January 1949. The *Guomindang* garrison in Beijing surrendered without a fight. Throughout 1949 fighting continued and the PLA moved relentlessly forward driving Chiang's remaining forces before them. In May 1949 Shanghai fell and Chiang, with a handful of forces, escaped from the Chinese mainland to the island of Formosa (Taiwan).

On 1 October 1949 Mao proclaimed China a people's republic. The spot he chose was Tiananmen Gate in Beijing, where imperial edicts had been proclaimed for centuries. Victory had been costly and was followed by a long and difficult recovery.

◁ Nationalist troops waiting to be evacuated from Shanghai to South China, 1949. When Shanghai fell thousands of landowners, businessmen and other rich people fled the country. Chiang gathered up as much treasure as he could and fled to Formosa (Taiwan) with other *Guomindang* members and a few loyal troops.

Communist bases

Mao believed that political change in China could only come through the peasants. During the 1930s the communists set up bases in the country-side. Once a base was established, selected leaders would be sent to neighbouring areas to set up new bases.

China under Mao

Modernisation was the order of the day after the communists achieved power. However, there were many obstacles for them to overcome.

△ Mao Zedong was revered as a hero and posters of him appeared on walls throughout China. Mao criticised the Soviet leader Stalin for the cult of personality but in fact he encouraged the same process himself.

The communists had pledged to modernise China, but before they could set about doing this they had to rebuild houses, factories, roads and railways which had been destroyed after years of fighting. Mao asked for aid from the Soviet Union – a communist ally. Stalin offered little aid at first, since the Soviet Union had also endured massive losses during the Second World War but in 1950 a Sino-Soviet Alliance was signed. The United States still supported the beleaguered *Guomindang* in Taiwan who represented China in the United Nations.

Reforms in land and industry

Already during the last phases of the civil war Mao had allowed a campaign to "clean" the countryside, using terror. Once in power, the communists set about reforming land ownership. The communists took land away from landowners and rich peasants. They divided it and gave plots to poorer peasants. It was a violent process and between one and two million landowners died.

This was followed in 1954-56 by a process known as collectivisation. Families (200 or more) joined together to form large collective farms, where tools and equipment could be shared. The land was owned by the collective. The income of each person was calculated according to how much work was done on the collective farms. By 1957, 97 per cent of peasants were organised into collectives.

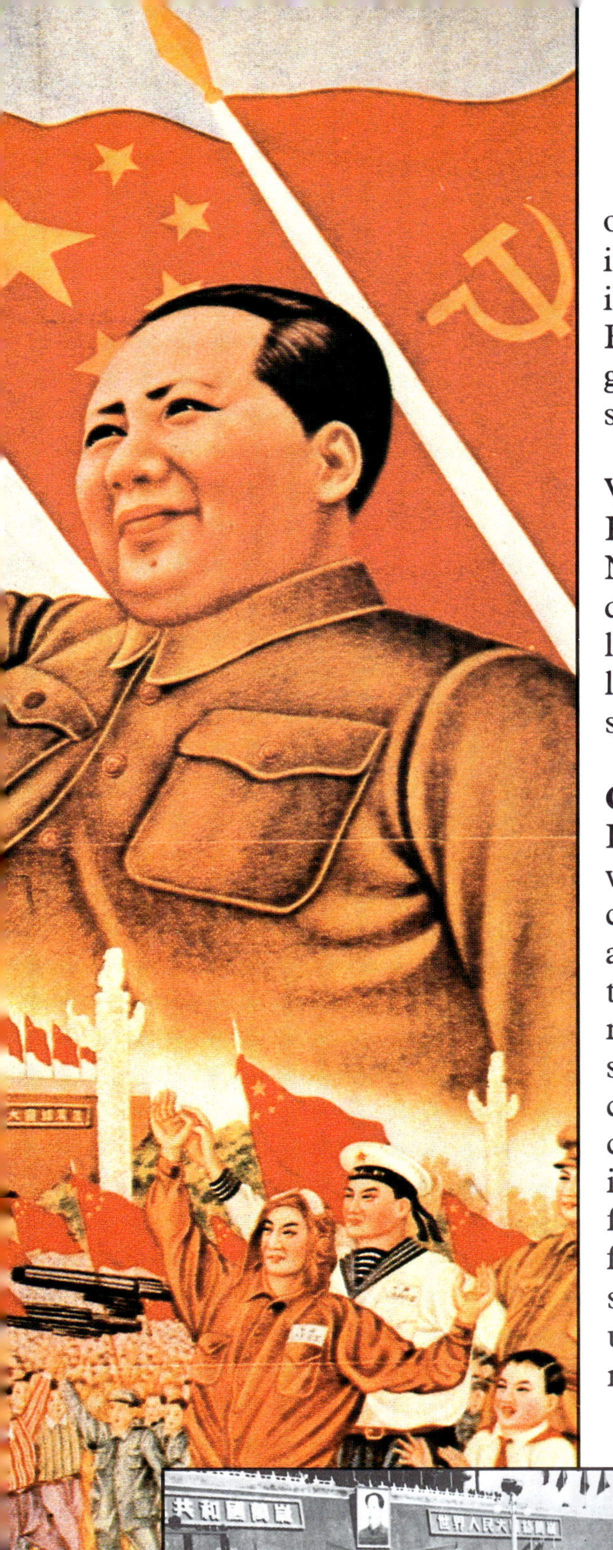

Industry was also re-organised and by 1952, 83 per cent of it was nationalised. That meant it no longer belonged to individuals but was owned by the state. By 1956 most of industry was nationalised. Following the Soviet example, Five Year Plans were launched to encourage economic growth. Money was put into building up heavy industries, such as, iron, steel, coal and cement.

Meanwhile China had become involved in the Korean War, coming to the aid of communist North Korea. North Korea had invaded South Korea in June 1950. The United Nations (UN) had sent in forces (mainly US troops) to defend South Korea. Mao decided to intervene when it looked like the UN troops might cross into China. The war lasted from 1950-53. Hundreds of thousands of Chinese soldiers died fighting a foreign war.

Communist rule

In the 1954 constitution, power was supposed to be shared with other parties and non-party individuals, but in fact the communist ruling group was in control. Central and local administration was haphazard and enforced decisions through massive propaganda campaigns. Conducted in a military fashion these campaigns seemed almost too successful. It was enough for Mao to praise one particular collective and all the others, despite geographic and climatic differences, would imitate it. Still wages and inflation were under control and there were no large-scale famines or epidemics. There were successes too. Armies of flood-fighters had prevented a great flood in 1954, public sanitation had been improved, health clinics had been set up in the countryside and the new, simplified script meant more and more people were learning to read.

◁ In 1950 soldiers celebrated the communist victory by parading through Tiananmen Square in Beijing. Tiananmen Square is the largest square in the world and is situated south of the Forbidden City, which is where the emperors used to live.

The propaganda campaign

Mao now decided he wanted to find out what the Chinese people thought about his rule. He thought the communists could learn from criticism. Mao made a speech which urged the Chinese to "Let a hundred flowers bloom, and a hundred schools of thought contend". This was an ancient Chinese saying. He was soon shocked by the responses.

Peasants claimed to be oppressed and almost as starved as they had been in the past; workers complained about political managers' incompetence and miserable wages. Educated people were bitter about the lack of freedom. As hostile posters, meetings and newspaper articles criticised Mao's rule, many communist leaders thought the campaign was a mistake. It seemed that 30 per cent of Chinese were pro-communist, 30 per cent anti- and the rest indifferent as they could not recognise the difference between the old and the new. Mao concluded that he had to change the people's ideas and gain more support for communism.

△ Deng Xiaoping was one of the casualties of the Cultural Revolution. He had been with Mao on the Long March and was known to be a moderate in favour of economic reforms. In 1966 Mao's Red Guards called him a "capitalist roader" and he was publicly humiliated. He was a survivor and after 1973 was able to regain some of the important positions he had held before the Cultural Revolution.

The Great Leap Forward

In 1958 a great propaganda campaign launched the Great Leap Forward. Its aim was to take China from socialism into communism – where the people would control their factories and land. The aim was to transfer industry from the cities to the villages. This was to be done by organising large collective farms of 5,000 or more families, known as communes. These would act as a political and economic unit and run their own clinics, schools and public services.

As the campaign gathered momentum, it became clear that it was opposed by some communist leaders, such as Peng Dehuai, as well as some peasants and workers. Markets were closed down and people in the country were forced into huge communes of 40,000 people. Within these groupings income was to be distributed equally. People from the country were also sent away to work in factories to increase industrial development.

At the same time the Soviets decided to pull out of China. They had been providing some aid to China under the 1950 Sino-Soviet Treaty but there were many differences between the Chinese and Soviet versions of communism. The Soviets had previously agreed to give China the atomic bomb, now they went back on their promise. China lost Soviet economic aid and Soviet scientists and engineers went back home. Moreover the Great Leap Forward coincided with the worst famines in years in which some 20 million died.

△ At the age of 73 Mao swam down the Chang Jiang River to prove that he was fit and healthy.

Mao's reaction

Faced with another failure, Mao responded in an unexpected way. He argued that the failures were due to several factors: party officials, known as cadres, lacked revolutionary spirit, were lazy and as corrupt as previous state officials had been under the emperors. He also thought land should not be in private hands and workers were being converted into capitalists by the incentive schemes to make them work harder.

Although Mao was chairman of the Communist Party, he realised that power was slipping from his hands: Liu Shaoqi controlled the state and Deng Xiaoping was general secretary of the Communist Party. Curiously Mao failed to realise he had lost the revolutionary spirit and was acting like an ageing emperor.

The Cultural Revolution

In 1966, Mao swam some 24 km down the Chang Jiang River to prove to all Chinese that his body was sound. Then he launched the Cultural Revolution to stir up revolutionary fervour among the people. At massive rallies held in Tiananmen Square, he encouraged young students to be the vanguard of the revolution. They put on red arm bands and formed Red Guard units. Schools and universities were closed down.

At first the Red Guards criticised their teachers and the cadres in the institutions. Then some two million Red Guards from all over China were told to start criticising local party leaders and set up new local organisations. Most of the Red Guards were teenagers from secondary schools and for two years (1966-68) they spread the Cultural Revolution throughout China. But they also stormed universities, burned books, denounced those they saw as traitors, imprisoned party men and created civil war conditions. The Red Guards started fighting each other as they could not agree on how to set up new structures. They also started attacking the army.

In 1968 when clashes became violent and widespread, Mao called in the army to break up the most unruly Red Guards. The PLA had to intervene to restore public

◁ Red Guards march through Beijing in January 1967. Red Guards were groups of school and other students. They were instructed by Mao to get rid of all "bourgeois" and "imperialist" relics. The Red Guards wanted to change everything from street names to how things were run by local party officials.

services and reopen the schools. It set up a network of revolutionary committees to take control of areas where local government had been destroyed. Lin Biao's army appeared to be running the country.

Mao also had to struggle to reassert his leadership of the Communist Party. But the Cultural Revolution, as it was called, went on and on. Millions of young city dwellers were sent to the countryside to learn to live "real lives" from the peasants. Many political leaders simply disappeared – Liu died in prison. Deng was purged during this period and his son was permanently disabled when students threw him out of a window. It is now thought that one million people were killed during these upheavals and 100 million were treated illegally. These figures are vague and were supplied by later communist leaders.

However, there were other disturbing events taking place. In 1964 the Chinese had tested an atom bomb. The Soviet Union continued to see China as a threat to its security and there was a long-standing dispute between the two over border territories. In 1969 Chinese and Soviet troops began to fight over some mid-stream islands in the Ussuri River region in northern China. There were heavy casualties on both sides as tanks moved in. It looked as though there might be war between the communist giants but the affair fizzled out. The Chinese realised that their armies were probably no match for the Soviet Union's and they had to rethink their foreign policies. The border dispute was officially settled in 1989.

▽ Red Guards were encouraged to travel across China "exchanging experiences" and "learning from the peasants". Chinese soldiers were also sent to work in the fields and learn about the countryside. Mao said "Society was the biggest university".

△ The US President Richard Nixon and his wife were entertained by Zhou Enlai in Beijing, February 1972.

▽ In January 1975 Zhou Enlai outlined the way forward. He said that by 2000 China would achieve the "modernisation in agriculture, industry, defence and science and technology".

Friendship with the United States

The possibility of war provoked additional turmoil in China, which was already in the throes of the Cultural Revolution. Armies were transferred to the north and even the civilian population was forced into this war activity. In neighbouring Vietnam the Americans were fully engaged in the civil war between the south and north. Mao was then forced into the most remarkable change of friendship and alliance. In 1971, the US Secretary of State, Henry Kissinger, visited China and prepared the ground for a US-Chinese treaty, which was signed a year later by President Richard Nixon. The People's Republic of China also became a member of the United Nations. The door was now open to the outside world.

This new friendship stunned the world. The Soviet Union was considerably weakened by it, for in the event of a war it would have to fight on two fronts, western and eastern. But in return the United States and Western Europe had to develop economic ties with China. Japan quickly signed a treaty with China and yens began to pour in to update industry. More immediately the Chinese bought 30 complete industrial plants from the United States, worth some $2,000 million.

The Four Modernisations

This change of alliance completely reversed Chinese policies. The Cultural Revolution took a swing to the right. Zhou Enlai, who was a skilful mediator between rival tendencies in the party, had survived all the policy changes and had served as foreign minister and prime minister. His role was to explain and interpret communist policy for the party. He now began to outline how he saw China developing in the future.

In January 1975 despite being very ill with cancer, he addressed the Fourth National People's Congress and presented the "Four Modernisations". New, more modern ways were to be found to run agriculture and industry; the stress would be on science and technology; and to make these reforms acceptable he also proposed the modernisation of the armed forces.

The speech was Zhou's last public appearance. He died a year later. Meanwhile the party leadership began to struggle over who would succeed Mao. Then in the summer of 1976, months after Zhou's death, Mao finally died at the age of 83. It was now up to his successors to find a way of modernising China.

Deng takes over

Under Deng, China has enjoyed an economic revolution as enterprise and foreign trade have stimulated economic growth. The demand for political reform has also grown.

△ Hua Guofeng succeeded Mao as chairman of the Communist Party in 1976. One of his first actions was to arrest the Gang of Four. He said that China would "continue the revolution". He appeared alongside Mao in street posters. However he was not as skilful as Deng at arguing over what was Mao's "correct line" and in June 1981 was replaced as chairman.

The struggle to succeed Mao Zedong as leader of China began well before his death. Lin Biao, who was to be Mao's successor, was eliminated in 1971. Lin allegedly died when his plane mysteriously crashed, while trying to leave China for the Soviet Union. That left two factions struggling for power in China.

Rivals for power

Deng Xiaoping and his protege, Hu Yaobang, wanted to modernise China through economic reforms. They wanted to follow Zhou's policies.

The other faction seeking power was the Gang of Four (Mao's wife – Jiang Qing, Wang Hongwen, Zhang Chunqiao and Yao Wenyuan). They wanted the Cultural Revolution to continue and to change China by attacking "class enemies" and educating the people. While Mao was still alive he supported them and in April 1976 he had Deng dismissed from all party offices. The Gang of Four blamed Deng for the rioting in Beijing in Tiananmen Square following Zhou Enlai's death. Hua Guofeng, who had been responsible for security, became Acting Prime Minister and a few months later, on Mao's death, became chairman of the party.

△ In 1976 the Gang of Four were arrested but they were not tried until four years later. They were accused of plotting an armed rebellion and of torturing and killing people. Jiang Qing's defence was that she followed Mao's instructions. They were sentenced to death but this was changed to life imprisonment.

The new party chairman

This was a very surprising outcome to the succession struggle. Hua then surprised the world even further. One month after his succession he had the Gang of Four arrested and imprisoned. Deng kept in the background for another year as he tried to increase his power. Hua was a skilful politician but he was criticised by other leaders for failing to improve people's living standards and keeping too much money in the state's hands. By 1978 Deng had established his ascendancy. Hua remained in power until 1981, when he was sent to "rest and learn".

In 1978 Deng became vice-prime minister and deputy chairman. He was the most influential Chinese leader, but he did not have the top jobs in either the state or the Communist Party. He dominated Chinese politics and policies for the next 12 years but he still faced opposition within the party leadership and there were many occasions on which he had to back down over economic reforms.

Deng's policies

There were three main points in Deng's policies. Firstly, he followed Zhou's Four Modernisations policy. Secondly, he wanted economic reforms, such as, the peasants farming land on a contract system, also known as a responsibility system. By allowing them to make money from their work, they would produce more. He thought small-scale industries, such as, basket weaving workshops in rural areas, should be encouraged. He also was in favour of a market economy, where individuals could get richer from their own work.

Thirdly, he wanted an open-door policy, that is, the opening up of China. He wanted close co-operation with the West to bring money into China. Since 1977 Japanese, American, German, French, Italian and even British financiers and industrialists have invested in China, developed its industry and tapped its natural wealth. In addition to this there were to be cultural and academic exchanges, so that for example dance companies, theatres and professors would visit other countries and *vice a versa*. In 1985 Deng said "unless you are developing the productive forces and raising living standards, you cannot say that you are building socialism."

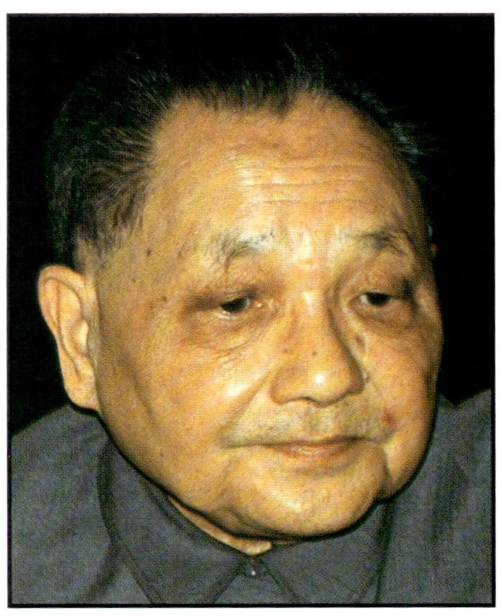

◁ Deng took two years after the death of Mao to gain the upper hand within the Communist Party. He believed in opening up China to foreign trade and increasing society's wealth.

The Fifth Modernisation

The idea of "the Fifth Modernisation" – greater freedom and more democracy – was first put forward in a poster on a Beijing wall in December 1978. The poster appeared on Democracy Wall in Tiananmen Square. The idea behind the campaign was that democracy would lead to more socialism. If people were allowed to criticise party leaders and elect party officials, things would improve.

The posters were read mainly by intellectuals and students. When as a result of the poster campaign, students became restless in 1978-79, Chinese security forces intervened and took away posters they did not like. Leaders of the poster campaign, including Wei Jingsheng, were arrested and imprisoned.

Deng's achievements

After the chaos of the Cultural Revolution it is possible that any reform programme would have met with success. But this does not do justice to Deng, who contributed a great deal to China's development.

The Chinese people enjoy a better standard of living. Modern technologies are widely available: radios and television sets, sewing and washing machines, watches and bicycles and even video recorders are accessible to many. More meat is being eaten – an average of 13 kg per person per year compared with 8 kg in 1978. House building is slowly catching up with need. Education is universal but sometimes children are kept away from schools to help with farming. However some enterprising peasants and businessmen are too wealthy compared to the rest, and the move of people from the countryside to the cities has lead to unemployment among some workers. By the late 1980s China had indeed gone through a remarkable change.

All this impressive economic progress leaves unanswered an important question. How far can a communist country go when introducing economic reforms? This remains to be seen. China now resembles the other rapidly developing countries in Asia, such as South Korea and Singapore.

During 1979, China got entangled in another foreign war. The People's Liberation Army proved it was an ineffective force in strikes against North Vietnam. It was then modernised with Western-imported arms. In October 1987, March 1988 and March 1989, the PLA killed thousands of unarmed Tibetans who were demonstrating against Chinese rule. This did a lot of damage to China's image abroad as a peaceful, modernising country.

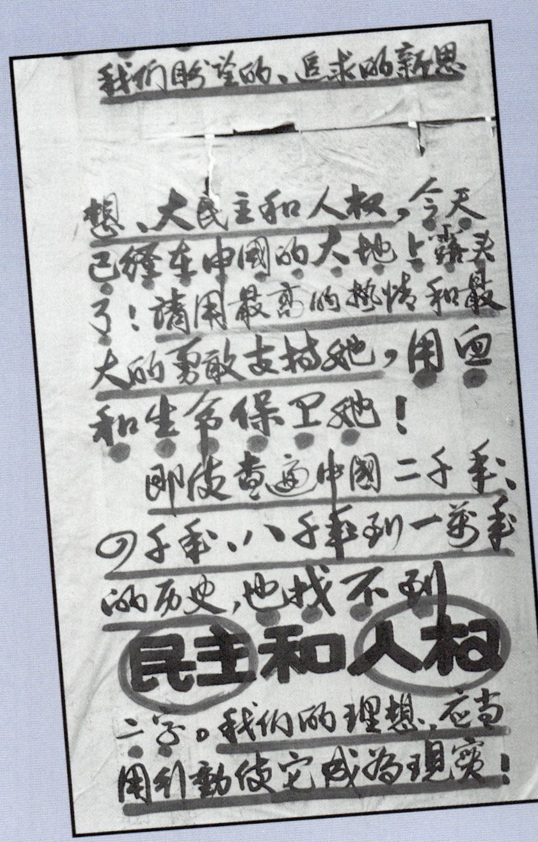

△ One of the posters that was pasted onto the wall facing Mao's mausoleum in Tiananmen Square in November 1978. The first posters that appeared on Democracy Wall criticised the leadership of Hua. They were followed by a stream of grievances about the state of the country. Some were brought into Beijing from outlying areas, complaining about decisions taken in Beijing. Unofficial magazines also appeared on the streets containing poems and short stories. Some even attacked Deng Xiaoping. After a few months, the communist leadership arrested some of the leaders of this protest and they were sentenced to imprisonment.

The Soviet example

Since 1985 the new Soviet leader, Mikhail Gorbachev, had been trying to change the communist system in the Soviet Union. When he became general secretary of the Communist Party, it was obvious that the Soviet economy was in a state of near collapse. It needed major restructuring (*perestroika*). The economy had to be re-organised so that it produced goods that people wanted and not goods that the central planning commission had ordered. This was to be a long-term process. Gorbachev knew he needed to get the people to support his reforms and one way to do this was give the people more freedom. The Soviet Union began to allow its people basic human rights: the right to speak in public; free speech on television and radio, in newspapers and magazines; the freedom to protest and demonstrate in the streets. In fact his political reforms were far more successful than the economic reforms.

By 1986 it seemed obvious to Deng that if China was to succeed in the economic sphere, then there would have to be political reform. He even stated that "As economic reform progresses, we deeply feel the necessity for changes in the political structure." The emphasis was on a very gradual move towards democratisation but no one was quite sure what changes he had in mind.

▽ Workers on a building site. With an expanding population, it is important that China builds enough flats and houses for the people. Unfortunately even with a massive building programme there is still overcrowding. Most city dwellers only have six square metres to live in.

Tourism
From the years 1982-85 tourism in China increased by more than 20 per cent each year. Tourists could travel without permission to more than 470 cities, towns and countries. Nearly 27 million foreigners visited China in 1987. This represented a lot of foreign currency coming into the country. New hotels have been built and services developed for foreign visitors. A Kentucky Fried Chicken was even opened near Tiananmen Square!

The democracy crisis

Deng's economic reforms encouraged a more liberal atmosphere in China. In May-June 1989 students began to demand political change and democracy but an inflexible state responded by bringing the army in to put them down.

By the late 1980s Deng's system of making economic reforms without making any real political reforms was being challenged. Hu Yaobang, the general secretary of the Communist Party, threatened to launch an anti-corruption drive within the party and the army. Six months later he lost his job because he had failed to control student demonstrations in December 1986 and January 1987. Deng remained in power even though at 82 he was 11 years older than Hu.

However, it looked likely that Hu's successor, Zhao Ziyang, would continue to press for political reforms, though in a more cautious way. After all, the communists in Poland and Hungary were changing their systems in order to succeed in the economic sphere. Above all, Gorbachev's introduction of *glasnost* (openness – meaning more freedom) in the Soviet Union went far ahead of

△ In February 1989 US President George Bush entertained the Chinese communist leaders at a Texas-style barbeque at the Sheraton Hotel in Beijing. He also invited Fang Lizhi, a critic of the Communist Party, to attend but security forces made sure he did not get to the banquet.

▷ Hu Yaobang was a leading reformer and one of the first senior communist leaders to wear a Western suit. After six years in power, he was forced to resign in January 1987.

anything the Chinese Communist Party was thinking of.

In the meantime China's economic reforms were beginning to run into problems. In the spring of 1988 Zhao and Deng decided that the state should stop fixing the price of goods but that producers of goods should work out their own prices and sell their goods on the open market. Within six months this policy had produced massive inflation such as China had not seen since before the communists took power. People bought goods because they were afraid they would not be able to afford them if the prices went up. By the end of 1988 price controls were brought back in and Zhao suffered an immense loss of face. His reforms had not worked. Li Peng, the adopted son of Zhou Enlai, who took over economic policy, became more important and criticised the "shortcomings and mistakes in our guidance".

△ Deng's economic reforms have meant that there are many more consumer goods available. Rising prices in 1988 led to panic-buying in the larger Chinese cities.

Foreign visitors

In February 1989 the newly elected president of the United States, George Bush, visited China representing the most powerful Western democracy. Western press and TV media were in full strength in Beijing and stayed on to cover further visits and events. Since Gorbachev was also coming to visit China for a summit meeting with Deng, many Chinese must have felt stimulated by this opportunity to ask the question "why shouldn't there be more freedom and political reform in China?" in public. The open-door policy had given rise to a very liberal atmosphere in Beijing.

In April 1989, when Hu Yaobang's death became known, students all over China discussed Chinese problems: the corruption of party officials and the slow progress of democracy which Hu Yaobang was associated with. Corruption in government circles had long been a problem. Contracts for business were usually clinched with gifts or even cash payments. Although minor party officials were occasionally disciplined, the leading figures were not touched. Those in power were often accused of using their positions to get favours and money for their relatives. Deng was accused of allowing his disabled son to profit from his job as head of a disability commission. Zhao Ziyang, the architect of economic reforms, was also accused of letting his son get involved in corrupt business deals.

The activity on university campuses did not upset Deng or his fellow leaders. They thought that they would be able to show Gorbachev that China was also on the way to greater democracy. Even anti-communist posters on the famous Democracy Wall were tolerated and student discussions were permitted with the staff joining in.

The May Fourth Movement
When the 100,000 students marched on Hu's death, they were remembering previous student movements. On 4 May 1919 Chinese students had protested against the terms of a foreign treaty.

Demonstrations and unrest

One of the fundamental principles of democracy has always been the right to peaceful demonstration. The assembly of Beijing students decided to put this to the test by marching out of their campuses and assembling in Tiananmen Square in central Beijing to express their grief over Hu's death. This demonstration was not dispersed by the security police.

There followed other demonstrations against corruption and for greater democracy. At first they were timid and very peaceful. But when Western reporters zoomed in on them, they became excited, high-spirited and even rowdy. Several student leaders made their appearance on television. Eventually the students decided to occupy Tiananmen Square until Deng and the party leaders listened to their voices and satisfied their demands. Students from all over China poured in to join in the demonstrations.

One of the first petitions presented to the Party leadership included seven demands: firstly, clearing Hu Yaobang's name; going back on past campaigns; making known the incomes and assets of party leaders; free speech and a free press; more funding for education; increased wages for teachers and other intellectuals; and finally the right to hold demonstrations.

The hunger strike

Deng did not respond to these demands but ordered the government-controlled newspaper, the *People's Daily*, to print a statement which laid down his position "This is a planned conspiracy and turmoil ... if we do not resolutely check this turmoil, our state will have no calm days". Nonetheless the students continued to stay in Tiananmen and ask for democracy. At this point several "leaders" emerged among the students. One was a history student at Beijing University, Wang Dan. He had arranged seminars on democracy and he was involved in the demonstrations from the start. Another "leader" was Wuerkaixi, an education student from Chinese Turkestan. Chai Ling was a psychology student. She became "commander-in-chief" of the students.

On 4 May the students held another mass demonstration to commemorate a previous protest by students in 1919. The students drew up a new petition. On 12 May, when the party leaders did not respond, 400 students decided to go on hunger strike. The occupation of the square was organised, tents were put up, students were coming and going in "shifts" and the hunger strikers were attended by medical staff. Their numbers swelled to 2,000.

▽ Students demonstrating in Tiananmen Square, May 1989. Since the May Fourth Movement, Tiananmen Square has been the traditional place to hold political rallies. Students were behind the Democracy Wall campaign in 1978. In September 1985 students marched to Tiananmen Square to protest against trade with Japan.

▽ A student leader shouting slogans in Tiananmen Square, May 1989. One of the slogans was "Down with the emperor", referring to Deng Xiaoping.

△ The Soviet leader, Mikhail Gorbachev arrives at Beijing airport to be greeted by President Yang Shangkun, 15 May 1989. The welcoming ceremony should have taken place in Tiananmen Square but it was hastily rearranged at the last minute. Gorbachev's visit to China was the first meeting of Soviet and Chinese leaders for 30 years.

The leaders' indecision

From 15-18 May, Gorbachev's visit to Beijing passed off without much incident, although there were many changes to his schedule. He was not allowed to go near Tiananmen Square, because of the occupation and had to approach the Great Hall of the People in the square through back streets. In Shanghai he found that the demands for Chinese democracy were widespread. In fact there had been student demonstrations in Guangdong, Hunan, Hubei, Shaanxi and Sichuan provinces.

At this point Prime Minister Li Peng and Zhao Ziyang came to see the mass protest and "feel" the desire for democracy among the young. Zhao cried publicly and blamed himself for not coming to meet the protesters sooner. Li was unimpressed and probably decided that it was time to repress the students. Afterwards Li claimed that the leadership could not decide on how to repress it. Apparently the security forces had no tear gas, rubber bullets or sufficient numbers of water cannon. In the end the leadership decided that the People's Liberation Army would have to do the job. However, there were no reliable forces available. Zhao was put under house arrest and President Yang Shangkun was put in charge of operations. He turned to the 27th Army, based in Shijiazhuang, Hebei province and composed mainly of poorly educated country men. Yang also had personal ties with this army: his brother was a political commissar there and the chief of staff was another relative. The 27th Army was then transferred to Beijing.

▷ On 30 May students from the Central Institute for Fine Arts erected a 30-foot tall plaster statue of a woman holding a flame. It was called the "Goddess of Democracy" and it was placed at the northern edge of Tiananmen Square where it faced Mao's portrait. The Beijing students probably got the idea for their goddess from Shanghai students who placed a model of the Statue of Liberty outside local government buildings.

△ During April and May there were also student demonstrations in Shanghai. The first large demonstration took place on 2 May, when 6,000 students marched to the People's Square.

Martial Law

On 20 May Li Peng announced that martial law was being introduced. This meant demonstrations, boycotts and strikes were banned. Speeches were forbidden as was the spreading of rumours. No one was allowed to hand out leaflets or organise petitions. The party leadership thought they could intimidate the students by declaring an emergency and getting the 27th and the 38th Army to encircle Beijing. But after a few days of dithering the students returned in force to the square and were joined by Beijing workers and citizens.

Among the students there was confusion. Some wanted to leave the square and continue to protest in a different way. But after the "final" rally many students decided to stay on. On 30 May, to boost their spirits the students built a "Goddess of Democracy" and placed it on the northern side of Tiananmen Square. Nearly 100,000 saw the spectacle but once it was over there were fewer than 5,000 left in the square.

On 3 June the army then decided to send lorries and buses of troops into Beijing. However, they were stopped by people standing in the road and stranded soldiers either deserted or were disarmed and even maltreated by passers by. Young men danced on the buses. Several attempts to use the underground and overground railways to get troops into Tiananmen Square also failed. Rumours were rife that the "good" 38th Army would not allow the "bad" 27th Army to move against the students. The rumours turned out to be wrong.

Showdown

On the night of 3 June some 50,000 armoured troops of the 27th, 28th and 63rd Armies received the final order to take the city and the square by assault. As they advanced towards Beijing from four different directions, the population made it clear that, though unarmed, it would not yield to brutal armed force. Buses were used as barricades to slow down the advance. Then at 11.35pm the soldiers started firing at the barricades. At midnight the convoy of troops resumed its progress.

In the early hours of 4 June the tanks reached the square and began their task of clearing it. The students gathered round the Goddess of Democracy in a last gesture of defiance. The soldiers then charged the unarmed students using their automatic weapons. Anyone on the streets was a target for the soldiers and casualties poured into the hospitals. The occupants of houses and flats nearby were shot accidentally. It is thought that some 1,000 people died in the chaos of the 3-4 June, though this may well be an underestimate. A government official put out a statement claiming that only 23 students died together with a few hundred troops. The democracy movement was crushed.

▽ Disturbances in Beijing lasted for several days. The sight of the PLA harassing students shocked many Chinese.

△ The day after the massacre a young factory worker held up column of tanks driving out of Tiananmen Square. Friends had to pull the man away.

△ Workers prepare Tiananmen Square for the 40th anniversary of the setting up of the People's Republic. This happened in October, only a few months after the massacre that shocked China and the world.

Aftermath

For 12 days no one was allowed into the square while the evidence of the bloodshed was cleared away. Still protests continued, but only on a very small scale. After the army's terror campaign security troops moved in to arrest "troublemakers" nationwide. Many people, including the student leaders, were arrested, others succeeded in escaping abroad. Fang Lizhi, a leading critic of the government, found refuge in the US embassy. Many others were tried by military court and some were executed. Human rights organisations estimate that some 10,000 people may have been arrested. There were real fears of civil war.

Foreigners panicked and were encouraged to leave Beijing and China to escape trouble. Universities were occupied by the army, which launched clearing up operations. The universities started teaching students again. However, to destroy the democratic movement among the students, all first year students throughout China will have to spend their time working in the country rather than learning in their lecture rooms.

Outside reaction

The whole world watched the events in China. The revulsion at the Tiananmen Square bloodletting was universal. Poland and Hungary condemned it outright, the Soviet Union was more diplomatic. Some countries refused to sell China any more arms – the United States, Great Britain, France and others. Others decided to suspend economic aid – Japan. World Bank loans were frozen. Since many foreigners have left China, many of the joint projects are also frozen. Foreign trade this year will be badly affected.

However the democracy movement does live on in foreign countries. Exiled students have set up the Federation for a Democratic China in Paris. The final irony of Tiananmen Square was that in November 1989 one of the student demands was achieved when Deng stood down from the leadership at the age of 85.

Above all, what happened in China has given communism a bad name, while it was trying to improve its image in the Soviet Union, Poland, Hungary and elsewhere. Western democracies will have to bear in mind this Chinese aboutface, when considering communist requests for economic aid. The bloody sacrifice for democracy's sake in Tiananmen, Beijing, should not be forgotten.

Chinese Politics

China has a communist system of government but its system is different from the Soviet Union's. Mao Zedong adapted the communist ideas of Karl Marx and Vladimir Ulyanov Lenin to China. Under the Soviet system the Communist Party is the only party allowed and it runs the country. The state owns all the land, industry, banking and other services.

Since China was mainly an agricultural country, Mao said the peasants were the the most important part of the system. He thought opposition to the Communist Party (of which he was head or chairman) should be allowed. If the peasants did not agree with the party's decisions then they should win. In practice the peasants did not often win over the party.

The Communist Party

The Communist Party runs the country. The government is separate from the party in name but in practice is dominated by the party.

The Communist Party is made up of 48 million people which is about four per cent of the total population. There are no elections in which the people can choose who will lead them. However there are a few local elections where people can choose who will run local administration.

The National Party Congress, rather than the party at large, chooses the Central Committee, which in turn chooses the Politburo and its Standing Committee and the General Secretary.

This diagram shows the relationships between the different parts of the government and the party. They are supposed to be separate but in practice this is not the case.

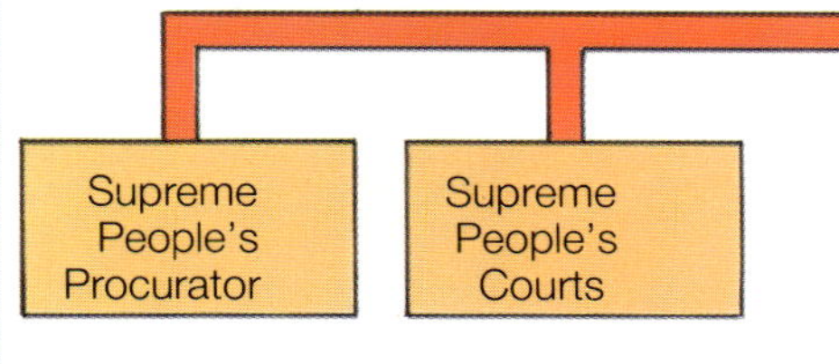

Structure of the government

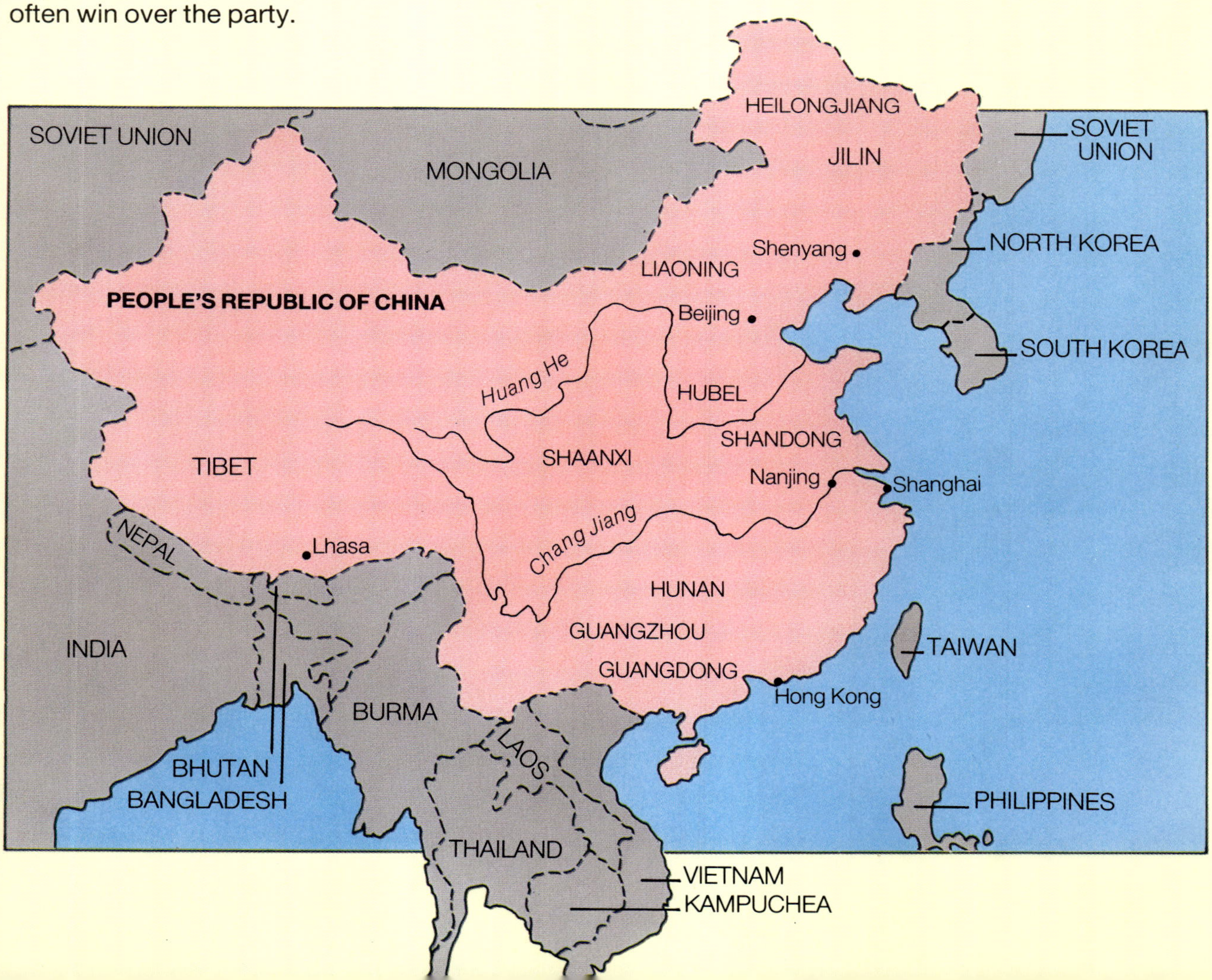

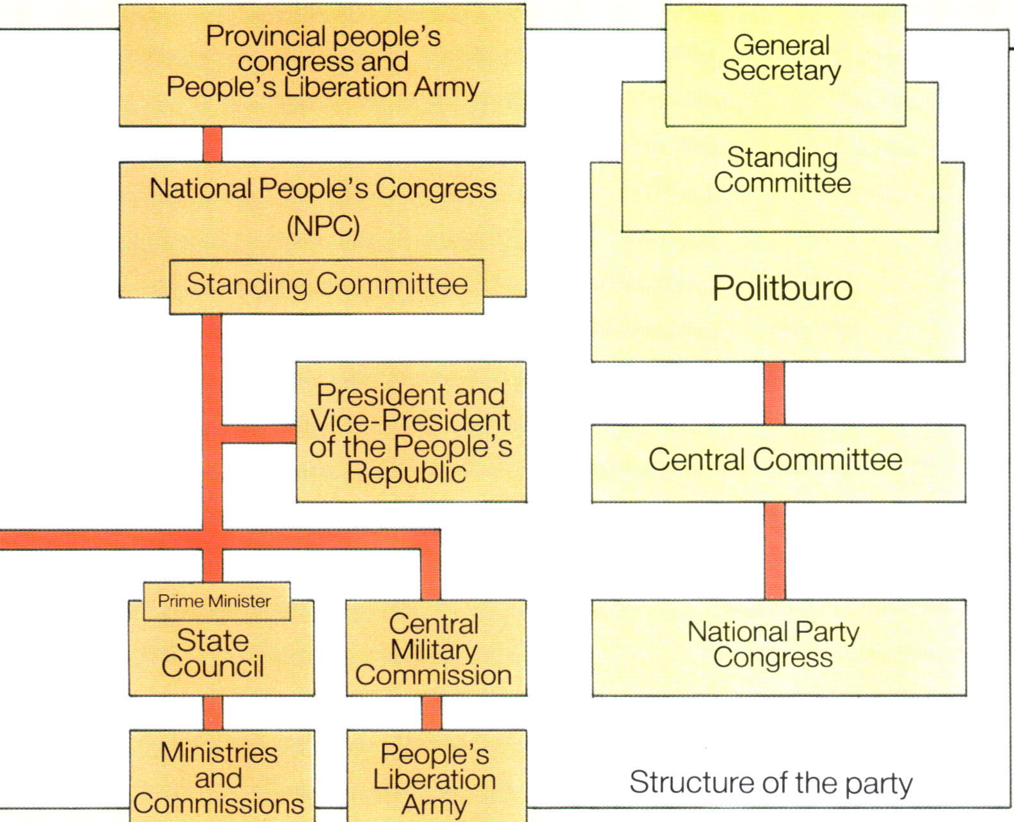

Structure of the party

These included the Economic Structural Reform Research Institute, the China Rural Development Research Centre, the Institute of International Studies of the China International Trust and Investment Corporation and the Beijing Association of Young Economists.

Many of the decisions about how to run the country are taken by the Standing Committee of the Politburo, which has about five members. The Politburo, the Central Committee and National People's Congress Standing Committee often merely ratify decisions taken by the Standing Committee.

The government
Those who serve on the National People's Congress (NPC) are chosen by provincial-level people's congresses and by the People's Liberation Army. The NPC works mainly through its permanent Standing Committee. The NPC chooses the prime minister, but normally on the recommendation of the Communist Party Central Committee. The Standing Committee also decides on appointments to the State Council on the recommendation of the prime minister. The NPC elects the President and Vice-President of the People's Republic of China, the Chairman of the General Military Commission and the highest legal figures. The NPC also passes new laws. In the last few years it has begun to play a greater role in policy discussion.

Other parties
There are other parties and groups but they have no power. They are represented on the Chinese People's Political Consultative Conference.

Think-tanks
In order to speed up the modernisation programme, the party leadership set up several think-tanks to work out new economic policies.

The army
This is still important as without its support the Communist Party would not be in power. There are 3.7 million people in the army and 300,000 in both the navy and air force.
The General Military Commission oversees the People's Liberation Army. The commission is responsible to the National People's Congress and its standing committee. The commission's chairman is elected by the National People's Congress. The army has lost prestige under Deng and defence spending has gone down.

Under Deng
When Deng took charge of the Chinese Communist Party, he announced that the party was in need of reform. In 1982 the party's propaganda chief produced a list of problems, including corruption and leaders' selfishness. Between 1982-87 the Central Discipline Inspection Commission tried to root out corruption but in fact it acted mainly against Gang of Four supporters. The most important party official who was dismissed was the Minister of Forestry, Yang Zhong. It was the corruption of party officials that fuelled demands for political reform in 1989.

China's economy

China was the world's leading iron ore producer in the 15th century. But it fell behind the rest of the world when the Industrial Revolution led to massive industrial development in Europe.

Today there is still a gap between China and the industrialised countries of Europe and the United States. In many ways it is a developing country. China is the world's third largest producer of coal after the United States and the Soviet Union. It also has large reserves of oil in the barren wastelands of the north-west and is the world's fifth largest oil producer. This means it is self-sufficient in both coal and oil and has begun to export petroleum products. China has large deposits of bauxite, uranium, tungsten and low-grade iron ore. It also has deposits of gold, silver and lead.

The biggest employer of Chinese people is still agriculture but industry does generate more GDP (the value of economic activity). The main industries are chemicals, textiles, metals and engineering. But much of the machinery and plant in use is still out of date.

China is the world's leading producer of wheat and rice. The main products grown in China are grain, rice, tea, soya beans, cotton, silk, tobacco, peanuts and fruit. Farmers also keep cattle, pigs, chickens and horses. Feeding such a large population has always been a problem and much of agricultural production is labour intensive. It also needs to be modernised.

Transport in China is well behind other industrialised countries. Many roads are little more than dirt tracks linking villages to markets. There are very few cars in China but there are public bus services.

Under Mao

After the communists came to power, Chinese agriculture and industry was re-organised. Mao stressed the need for China to be self-sufficient.

At first the peasants were given their own plots of land from 1950-53. Then they were encouraged to join agricultural co-operatives, which were then developed into collective farms. People in the country were also used for public works, like building flood barriers, dams irrigation ditches and other projects. In 1958 the collective farms became much larger people's communes. Farm workers were paid according to the number of points they had gained rather than how much they had produced.

Industry, banking and trade were nationalised and became state owned. In 1953 following the Soviet example, Five Year Plans were drawn up to set production targets. Central planning set out what each factory was supposed to produce. Taxes from agricultural produce were used to invest in heavy industry, like iron and steel.

The Great Leap Forward did not produce the required economic leap and in the early 1960s China's economy declined. During the Cultural Revolution, when the country was in turmoil, there were also economic problems.

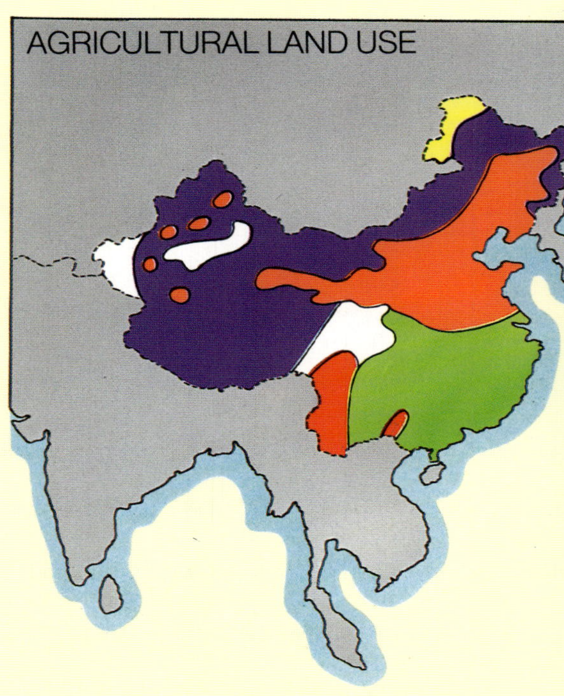

Bauxite
Lead
Gold
Zinc
Silver
Tin
Iron ore
Industrial areas

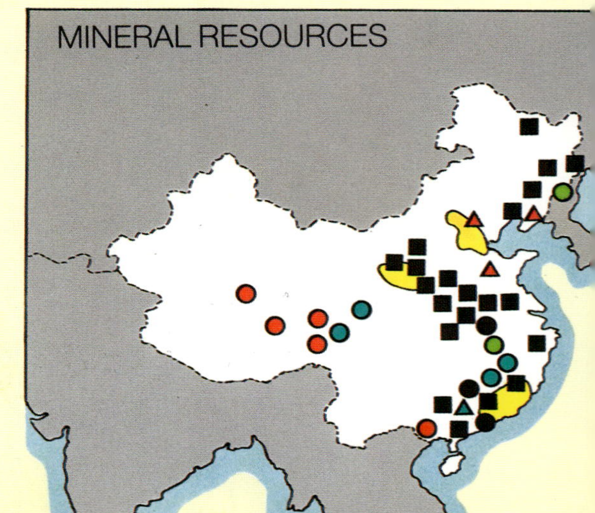

Deng's reforms

In the early 1970s trade with the United States opened up and the party reverted to trying to build up cash from agricultural produce to put into industry so living standards declined. By the time Deng took over the "Four Modernisations" policy was being pursued.

The new policies to achieve economic growth involved giving greater incentives to workers and opening China to foreign trade, investment and technology.

In 1979 a new responsibility system was introduced to improve agricultural output. Each household was contracted to produce a certain amount for the collective farm. The family could then sell any extra on the market. More land was given over for private plots. Farm production increased. Farm families also undertook sideline activities, such as, providing transport, raising chickens, forestry, producing handicrafts and many other activities. Some did very well out of the new system but those who were unable to work did not do so well – such as, the sick and the ill. The services which the communes had provided also declined.

Industrial reforms

Deng's reforms gave plant managers more responsibility. Instead of having quotas, managers were given loans and given greater freedom to produce goods which were needed locally. Specialised banks were set up to provide credit.

State industries were allowed to retain their profits. Under the new system they paid a tax to the government and had to compete on the market. Some factories paid bonuses to their workers so they would work harder. Co-operative enterprises were encouraged. More consumer goods were produced and people's living standards rose.

Four Special Economic Zones were set up, where foreign companies could take part in joint ventures. These were sited on the coasts and one was next to Hong Kong. The idea was that they would act as a half-way house between capitalist Hong Kong (which is under British control until 1997) and socialist China. The zones were very successful and more are being set up.

The results

For the last decade, China has enjoyed impressive economic growth. However there are still many economic problems. China still has an inadequate transport system. It has not always been able to import the new machinery it needs. Chinese workers have to learn how to use foreign technology. There has been a shortage of modern managers and skills. Meanwhile the population is still expanding and agricultural production has to keep pace with it.

▽ Steel workers near a furnace.

Chronology

In the 20th century China had been subject to civil war followed by the long process of reconstruction. Under the leadership of Mao for nearly 40 years, communist China enjoyed much progress and a few reverses. For the last ten years, China has known economic growth as the communist economic system has been reformed. In 1989 the pro-democracy movement was crushed.

1912 Establishment of the Republic of China.

1916 The warlord era.

1921 Chinese Communist Party founded in Shanghai.

1928 Chiang Kaishek forms the *Guomindang* government with its capital in Nanjing (Nanking); Mao Zedong sets up the Red Army.

1931 The Japanese Kwantung Army invades and occupies Manchuria.

1934-35 The Long March – the communist forces leave their Jiangxi base in southern China and march to establish a new base in Yanan in northwestern China.

1937-45 War between Japan and China.

1937-41 Temporary truce between Chiang and Mao.

1941-45 Second World War in the Far East; China enters the war on the side of the Allies – the United States, Soviet Union, Britain, France and others.

1945 Japanese defeated in the Second World War; Chinese Civil War begins.

1948 The communists capture the cities of Manchuria.

1949 The communists defeat the *Guomindang* and take Beijing in January; Mao Zedong proclaims the establishment of the People's Republic of China in Tiananmen Square, Beijing.

1950 Friendship Treaty signed with Soviet Union; China enters the Korean War in support of North Korea; the PLA invades Tibet.

1950-53 Land reform carried out.

1953 End of the Korean War.

1958 The Great Leap Forward begins.

1959 Uprising in Tibet suppressed; the Dalai Lama flees to India.

1960 The Soviet Union withdraws aid and the Sino-Soviet split becomes open.

1964 China tests an atomic bomb.

1966-76 Cultural Revolution in China.

1969 Border dispute with the Soviet Union.

1971 China gains a United Nations seat and becomes a permanent member of the UN Security Council; Lin Biao dies in a plane crash.

1972 US president, Richard Nixon, visits China.

1976 Deng dismissed; Mao Zedong and Zhou Enlai die; Hua Guofeng appointed Communist Party Chairman.

1978 Deng Xiaoping becomes the Republic's new leader.

1979 Democracy Wall protest is stopped; China signs trade agreements with the United States.

1980 Trial of the Gang of Four begins; Zhao Ziyang becomes Chinese prime minister.

1981 Hua Guofeng is replaced as chairman of the party by Hu Yaobang.

1987 Hu Yaobang resigns; Zhao Ziyang becomes general secretary of the party; demonstrations in Tibet suppressed.

1988 Li Peng confirmed as prime minister; inflation hits 20 per cent and price reforms stopped; demonstrations in Tibet suppressed.

1989 Hu Yaobang dies; Gorbachev visits China for Sino-Soviet summit; pro-democracy students killed in Tiananmen Square; Zhao Ziyang removed from office; Deng Xiaoping steps down from leadership; 40th anniversary of the People's Republic.

Glossary

Bourgeoisie the middle classes – shopkeepers, clerks, civil servants and others. It was used as a term of abuse during the Cultural Revolution.

Capitalism the economic system in which all enterprises are owned privately. Wealth or capital can be put to whatever use the individual wants.

Collectivisation the redistribution of land so that it is run by a collective farm. Teams of farm workers then ploughed, planted and harvested crops instead of individuals or families.

Communism the belief that all private wealth should be abolished and all things are held in common, that is, by the state. In practice the state decides who has money and fixes prices.

Cultural Revolution a mass revolutionary movement inspired by Mao Zedong in 1966. Its aim was to remove the established party organisation.

Democracy the political system where people have a say in choosing or electing their government.

Dynasty a line of kings or queens from the same family.

Fifth Modernisation the term used by Wei Jingsheng to describe democracy. He used it on a wall poster in 1978.

Four Modernisations the term used by Zhou Enlai to describe China's way forward. It involved the modernisation of agriculture, industry, defence and science and technology.

Gang of Four was the name given to the four members of the Politburo, who supported the Cultural Revolution and its aims. They were Jiang Qing (Mao's wife), Wang Hongwen, Zhang Chunqiao and Yao Wenyuan. They were arrested in 1976 and put on trial in 1980-81. They are now serving long jail sentences.

Glasnost the Russian word meaning transparency or openness which is used to describe the cultural and political openness in the Soviet Union under Gorbachev.

Great Leap Forward was started in 1958. It was supposed to make China's economy catch up with other industrialised countries and make the leap from socialism to communism. The peasants had to join large communes and industry was transferred from the towns to the villages.

Guomindang the Chinese Nationalist Party which ruled part of China from 1928 to 1949. It then transferred to Taiwan and has since been the ruling party there.

Imperialism the building of an empire by acquiring territory from other countries.

Land reform the redistribution of land so that the peasants are given their own plots. It took place in 1950-53.

Nationalism the belief that one's country should be allowed to govern itself and should not have foreign rule.

People's Liberation Army the Chinese communist army.

Perestroika restructuring – the word used to describe the Soviet attempts to reform the communist system.

Politburo the body of leading Communist Party members who take some of the most important decisions about running the country.

Red Guards the young people in schools and universities who took part in the Cultural Revolution.

Second World War a war fought between 1939 and 1945, mainly in Europe and the Far East, which involved many different countries. The principal opponents were Germany, Italy and Japan, who were fighting the United States, Britain, the Soviet Union, France and China.

Sino a prefix meaning Chinese.

Socialism the belief that wealth should be distributed more equally through taxes and that some industry should be owned by the state. It was seen as a stage between capitalism and communism. The Chinese Communist Party is trying to make China a socialist country. By that they mean the state controls and owns all industry and wealth.

Soviet originally meant a workers' council. Now it is used to describe the Soviet Union.

Index

Photographic Credits:
Cover and pages 8 bottom, 18-19, 20, 27 top and bottom and 29 bottom: Frank Spooner Agency; intro page: Barry Lewis/Network Photographers; pages 4-5 top and bottom,6 both, 7, 8 top, 9 both, 10-11, 12-13, 13, 14-15, 15 top, 16-17, 16 top, 17, 18, 23 bottom, 24-25, 25, 26, 28-29, 28 left and back cover: Topham Picture Library; pages 14 top, 19, 22-23, 23 right and 33: Rex Features; page 21: Laurie Sparham/Network Photographers.